# BASUSENA

*(An untold saga of Karna, the tragic hero of Mahabharat)*

# BASUSENA
*(An untold saga of Karna, the tragic hero of Mahabharat)*

## Hrushikesh Mallick

*Translated by*
## Gopa Ranjan Mishra

**BLACK EAGLE BOOKS**
Dublin, USA | Bhubaneswar, India

Black Eagle Books
USA address:
7464 Wisdom Lane
Dublin, OH 43016

India address:
E/312, Trident Galaxy, Kalinga Nagar,
Bhubaneswar-751003, Odisha, India

E-mail: info@blackeaglebooks.org
Website: www.blackeaglebooks.org

First International Edition Published by
Black Eagle Books, 2024

**BASUSENA**
*(An untold saga of Karna, the tragic hero of Mahabharat)*
by **Hrushikesh Mallick**

Translated by **Gopa Ranjan Mishra**

Original Copyright © Hrushikesh Mallick
Translation Copyright © Gopa Ranjan Mishra

All rights reserved. No part of this publication may be reproduced, stored in a retrieval system, or transmitted, in any form or by any means, electronic, mechanical, photocopying, recording or otherwise without the prior permission of the publisher.

Cover & Interior Design: Ezy's Publication

ISBN- 978-1-64560-559-1 (Paperback)
Library of Congress Control Number: 2024943077

Printed in the United States of America

To
Dhupanwita

Thanks to
Subash Chandra Mohapatra being associated with
the translation of this book.

# DOOR-SILL

Dear Readers,
You may cross the threshold or not, but it is the door-sill of this book and of that house where once lived Basusena alias Karna. Through this door, on that day, Kunti had gone out to end her maiden motherhood. Through this door, Hastina had once intruded into the day-to-day life of *sutaputra*. Putting a victory-mark on the forehead and saying goodbye, here stood *Brusali* for a long time, still and motionless, on the second day of a dark fortnight of one *Phalguna*. Longing for *Panchali* all his life and not getting her, the exhausted body of grief-stricken *Radheya* had rested upon the door-sil. Here only, a determined arrow had dreamt many a disordered dream, hoping to conquer *Arjuna*. This door-sill leads you into numerous corners of this book and that house, behind the scene.

Beyond the door-sill, the man who sits in a pensive mood, is none other but our dear, ever- adorable, Karna, full of vigor and virility. Injured in its encircled body, hissing in its expanded hood, but helplessly coiled under the dictates of its own fate. If adversity engulfs its grooming, how is genius responsible for its waywardness? If growth of personality is on a wrong path, how can a person be held responsible? If motherhood becomes a bait for selfish gains, why should the tender childhood be blamed for disowning it? Without having courage to confront, if love hides behind the futile hints, how can the beloved refrain from detestation? Upon a careful enquiry, many-layered answers emerge out of Basu's life. Has any poet or writer ever taken enough care to build up such a rare character of the world? I admit Vyasa brought the soil, converted some to the image he conceived and left a lot as raw-mud out of which Karna is being endlessly built yet, one after another. Much like a piece of art, a sculpture this creation is a continuous process.

In course of going through the contributions of my predecessors, I have noticed new ideas lighting up in my innermost consciousness, relating to the life of Karna while much more, I felt, lay in the dark. At times, it seemed Karna was like an enigma for ever – half visible, half hidden in a distant mist, despite industrious efforts of so many poets and writers. Though much is revealed, much remains hidden. Two deep wounds are there at the core of the heart – one is Kunti and the other is Draupadi. The agony of these wounds has hardly been detected yet.

The manner in which the conversation between Karna and the charioteer Salya has been presented in the Mahabharat and the subsequent writings, the ill intention to undermine the importance of Karna is hardly a secret. The glory of Karna, the great conqueror, extraordinarily generous, determined and true to his vow, has spread far and wide.

In the original Mahabharat, Karna has fallen a victim to both love and resentment of Vyasa. Enough and reasonable attention has not been given to the quiet emotional moments of Karna in the broad expanse of Mahabharat. Doing this was perhaps not possible.

While recounting the episodes of Ghosayatra at Dwaitaban and the cow-stealing in the kingdom of Birat, the creators of Mahabharat have shown excessive eagerness to exibit the cowardice of Karna on both the occasions. If it is a case of interpolation, well and good. Neither of the two was wars in the true sense nor had Karna taken leadership in either. Not only Karna but the whole Kaurav army including Duryodhan was not able to successfully counter the sudden surprise attack of Gandharvas at Dwaitabana and Arjuna's organized attack. At different points of time, contributions of different writers, let alone Mahabharat, no single Purana has been completely free from interpolation while recounting the greatness of Karna, like Parshuram being much earlier to the era of Mahabharat, Karna learning archery from him and the fatal curse that befell him, seems unreal. Since inclusion of such stories do not come in the way of presenting Karna in an uncharitable way, this figures in Basusena. Because Mahabharat is as much Purana as it is history. So symbolic use of lofty imagination is not to be considered a blunder if it does not affect the primary objective behind building a character or incident.

When observed closely, incidents like Draupadi's disrobing and the killings of Ghatotkacha and Abhimanyu, we are inclined to conclude that the raconteurs of the earlier versions of Mahabharat had decided, as it were, or having been blind followers of their more illustrious followers, have shown Karna's entanglement in these unpleasant happenings and never felt the necessity of going out of the bulky trunk of the episode. For which Karna could not be kept unaffected in these places.

The intense inner reality that exists again in the outskirt of these three visible happenings (mishaps) which Karna has experienced himself, can never be presented in a justifiable way unless one gets into it. In Basusena all possible efforts have been made, somewhere in direct, others in an oblique way, to capture the backdrop of all these incidents. However, to determine how far it has been successfully done is, it is to be admitted with all humility, beyond the poetic ability of this poet.

If there was exaggerated account of Karna (like the killing of his own son Bishikeshan by Karna himself to please Krishna, disguised as a Brahmin, Karna Parva – Sarala Das), so was the presentation only ludicrous incidents like a part of the stern oath that Karna took – giving up consumption of wine and non-veg food – keeping Arjuna's killing in mind.

To take decision to abandon certain food and drinks for life just in order to be able to vanquish Arjuna seems childish, especially for one whose nature was contrary to meanness and narrow-minded thinking. It is as if killing of Arjuna does not demand skill and competence in weaponry but only giving up food that is proper for warriors. To make such unsavoury remark at the royal assembly that Droupadi is a prostitute or that, provoked by Salya's unseemly behavior, using slanderous terms like Madra's women were addicted to drinks and were of degraded characters – this is not reliable, when we consider Karna's upbringing under the tender care of Radha and Adhiratha. If the manner in which Karna conducted himself was so mean, he would not have been addressed with much honour in such unprecedented way as 'Maharathi' by Krishna while he revealed the secrecy of his birth and the way he spoke to Arjuna referring to Karna. Even Bhishma, while he lay on the bed of arrow, was full of reverence for Karna. Even Krishna would not have reminded Judhisthir to offer the first oblation to Karna when the former offered oblations to those heroes and soldiers killed in the war, in the river Drusadvati. How can it be acceptable that the same Karna who did not speak a word even in the face of insults, more grievous than death, hurled at him at the time of aim-testing at Panchala in the court of Kauravas, would get so provoked by the exchange of words between a warrior and a charioteer ( Salya, maternal uncle in relation) that he would lose his balance of mind in extreme anger. If this is said to be an instance of exaggeration, it is not easy to establish such arguments as unfounded.

For more than a month I had been undergoing an agonizing feeling as to what name I should give my book to the verses on Karna I had published in different magazines. The name Karna put me in a dilemma. Should it be titled Karna or some other suitable alternative. Is Karna a name after all . A son either born from an unwed girl or had come out of an ear (according to Sarala Das) is called 'Karna' (an illegitimate child). So, the birth-name of this genius hero, the great son of Kunti was never Karna. Some say, Radheya came to be known as Karna after he gave away his earrings to Indra, cutting off his own ears. If this is accepted, then by which name was Karna known before this offering? Being afraid of public disgrace, Kunti had floated down the baby son in the river, soon after his birth. So, where was the scope for her to name the baby. After being rescued from the river, the birth-rituals of the nameless orphan was observed in the house of Adhiratha and, most probably, at that time he might have been named as Basu or Basusena. Since then, generation after generation, his successors got authority to use this title 'Sen' or 'Sena'. The name such as Susena, Prasena and Brusasena of Karna's sons indicate this.

Behind 'Basusena' lies long twelve years of my sleepless, studious poetic life. Yet, I haven't been able to keep this composition, as in most such compositions of the world, free from incompleteness. This strange character Karna is so unlike other characters in Mahabharat in the sense that after it is written in one way, it keeps revealing itself in many different ways before the person who conceives / designs it. As I begin to write the Introduction, after completion of the poem, a question strikes me what was the real motive behind Indra's begging earrings and defensive armour to Karna? To keep safe the life of his own son Arjuna or his frightened mind was occupied with the idea to wipe out the mortal identity of Kunti that was with Karna and to keep the true identity of Karna a mystery to Kunti for ever? Because many crucial decisions of Mahabharat including the possibility of a war depended on the disclosure of Karna's identity before Kunti. Had it been only begging Arjuna's life, why at all he had offered Karna such a weapon, in return, that was enough to destroy Partha.

In the whole Mahabharat, the character of Karna is such that one feels like looking at him in sheer astonishment And, that compels one to think where he begins and where does he end. I have not yet got the answer to which incidental alternative is true in the multi-layered life of Karna. While I was in the course of writing and after it was completed, I have felt it again and again – 'Can we finish all simply by writing', to quote Sarala Das. Still, it is expected, the apparent incompleteness of the book will be covered if unconditional support, free from jealousy, comes our way. This poet is not a Vyasa to assure one of getting such virtues one gets by donating Kapila Cow with its calf for the whole year. At least, if the book does not become an obstacle to the readers' fulfillment of achievable earthly and divine aspirations, it will be a festive pleasure for the poet.

**Hrushikesh Mallick**

# TRANSLATOR'S NOTE

While being the longest epic poem in the world in all of history, The Mahabharat is even grandeur when it deals with the nuances of human psychology in very morally ambiguous scenarios. And makes the audience question their own judgment and forces them to see the same scene from the perspective of different characters - all of them being "correct" from their vantage point and yet at war with one another.

In the case of Bhishma, it's a conflict of obligation towards the family he has sworn to protect versus his desire to do the righteous thing. Being forced to fight on behalf of his benefactors, Drona is forced to side against his favourite student. Even Duryodhana, the primary antagonist, who sets the war in motion with his selfish greed and arrogance, chooses a fair battle with Bhima when asked to choose any Pandava for a one on one combat. While Krishna, the God incarnate Himself, does not shy away from deception if it means that the final outcome is going to benefit humanity at large. If the Mahabharat has a message, it is that there is no single objective right or wrong in this world and every person has multiple layers and dimensions that make them act the way they do.

In this context one of the most multi-faceted characters in the whole epic is Karna. A prince and a demi-god, he is abandoned at birth for being born out of wedlock. His loving low-caste foster parents reveal to a young Karna that he is adopted - and it is this knowledge that shapes Karna's character throughout his life. Despite his immense skills, intelligence and wisdom he still cannot get over the fact that his own mother did discard him after he was born. This leads to a search of self-identity, which is heightened by the rebuke and insults he faces by his classmates for his being of a lower caste. He wants to experience a sense of belonging and acceptance and love from a society that is right next to him, yet feels forever out of his reach.

Finally when Duryodhana acknowledges his skill and befriends him and treats him as an equal, Karna feels validated for the first time in his life. And promises undying loyalty to his friend, no matter how dark a path his friend sets out on. This coupled with a desire for revenge towards Arjuna for numerous taunts in his childhood, shrouds the innate good in him. He joins in with the Kauravas and insults Draupadi and goads Dushasana into disrobing her in front of the court. He suggests an all out war against the Pandavas as a way of ending the long drawn hostility between the two families. Even when Kunti approaches him later, to reveal to him his real lineage and that he was about to go to war with his own siblings, he just says that while he has been longing for this moment his whole life, it came too late.

There is mention of Karna regretting his deeds and that his actions were meant to make Duryodhana happy. However, crippled by a lack of self-worth and blinded by his loyalty, it is hard to say if Karna himself was aware of the true reasons for his deeds. His life can be seen as a sad sequence of "what if"s. It is very likely that had his mother or society treated him better, he would have turned out to be one of the most virtuous characters in the Mahabharat. Probably there would not have been a war, which was his idea. Duryodhana would not have a close friend who could rival the Pandavas. If not for Karna's tragic life, maybe the times described in the Mahabharata would just have been another peaceful eventless era, not worth telling one of the greatest stories ever told.

With this as the glorious background about which Indian readers are fairly familiar, the poet Dr Hrushikesh Mallick has presented the character of Karna in a unique way. A distinguished poet in Odia, Dr Mallick has won many coveted awards including Central Sahitya Akademi award for his immense contribution to Odia literature. He is an erudite scholar in Indian epics. In Basusena, while retaining the qualities of Karna, befitting this character of epic grandeur, the poet has given a local flavour to the entire scenario from his birth, infancy, childhood, youth and the life and feelings of a true warrior so much so that the readers can relate themselves to the situations and circumstances in which Karna finds himself. In Karna we notice a blend of the human and the divine. In his distinctly poetic manner Dr Mallick has drawn the characters, especially Kunti and Karna, in a very impressive way. For instance, Kunti as a very young teenage girl, blessed with a divine mantra from the sage Durvasa ( chanting which she could call upon any god who would manifest himself and bless her with a son equal to him in glory). The impatient curiosity of youth makes Kunti test the efficacy of the mantra :

….Come forth
And in the lonesome darkness of my existence
Like my playmate of olden days
Cup my face
And with the mischievous pranks of adolescence

Close my eyes
Let my nipples swell with the lush green luxuriance
At the onset of *Ashadha*
...........
At such a turbulent stage of my life am I
That I can break down the barriers of father, mother
And elders.
And even the impediments caused
By the Lord himself.
...........
And in this very moment
I can crush into dust the past, present and the future
With my thunder-like desires....
With a mere drop of sperm
I can conceive in my womb
A whole host of universe
.......
With one solitary kiss
I can suck all the rivers, lakes and the seas
.......
I can challenge and shatter
The vigour and virility
Of the most austere celibate....
One who had all along been appearing as Kunti
Was really a coiled serpent
Which rises with the touch of a stick.

The verses run along with impassioned invocation to god and ends with the union of the Sun and Kunti, giving us an impression of a young girl, immersed in gross sensuality. That is what Kunti is undergoing but one has to appreciate the lofty, elevated language that the gifted poet has employed to give vent to the feelings of the girl, seized by passion.

When the battle is on, Karna is overcome by a sense of inferiority caused by the eulogy for Partha by Salya. And, like a common human being, he is too eager to listen to the slander of Partha :

......
But how I wish
I could hear someone slander against Partha
And Partha only…
Let Partha's slander
Come from all directions
From the premises of court
From the lips of children going to school
From the chirping of birds….
If I could hear the slanderous words
In the stealthy darkness
Coming from the neighbourhood of brothers…
From the songs of Yogis wandering
With begging-bowls
From the half-asleep, half-awake
Army-camp !....
To Partha's slanderer
I shall offer all my skills of archery
All my virtues of this life
And of previous lives, if needed
Rest of the kisses of my wife meant for me
Shall offer the span of my life….

Dr Mallick very artistically brings down Karna from a high pedestal and makes him speak like a commoner. Yet, the feelings are genuine and sincere. And, the readers are made to wonder at such verses stated above.

The whole of Basusena is replete with such verses. When I read the book in its original version (Odia), I felt impelled to translate it into English since I sincerely felt this great work richly deserves a wider audience. The wonderful command Dr Mallick has over Odia language and his way of presenting his thoughts in a form and style all his own sometimes defy translation. I have tried to make a modest attempt. I will be very happy if this translated version gives some moments of joy to the readers.

**Gopa Ranjan Mishra**

# 1

*(Durbasa departs from the royal guest-house of King Kunta Bhoja. Kunti worships
And invokes the Sun-god by virtue of the mantra offered to her by the Sage...)*

Oh! The Lord of Rays! I pray you to come....
Oh! Sun! I pray you to come...
Oh! The Lord of Light! I pray you to come...

From the heaps of sandals on the wooden seat
Worshipped by the guest
From the decaying shape of the wooden bound
From the vapour of the incense
From the highest peak of the mountain
From the unreachable height of the trees
From the space
From the hymns
From the shy, hesitant eruption of my passions
Come forth
And in the lonesome darkness of my existence
Like my playmate of olden days
Cup my face
And with the mischievous pranks of adolescence
Close my eyes.
Let my nipples swell with the lush green luxuriance
At the onset of *Ashadha*
And my maiden ear-base be rendered fertile
Like the earth of *Akshya Trutia*

At such a turbulent stage of my life am I
That I can break down the barriers of father, mother
And elders.
And even the impediments caused
By the Lord himself.
I can fling myself into the farthest corner
Of the most frightening thunder
The beating of my heart may be made from the flashes
Of the lightning that blinds the eyes.
I can give shelter to the violent breathing before death
In my nostril.
And in this very moment
I can crush into dust the past, present and the future
With my thunder-like desires
In the serene ambience of timelessness
With a mere drop of sperm
I can conceive in my womb
A whole host of universe
With the animates and inanimates
Worms and insects.

With one solitary kiss
I can suck all the rivers, lakes and the seas
Now I am such an earthquake
That I can shake and unsettle
The very base of existence
I can challenge and shatter
The vigour and virility
Of the most austere celibate
Built under the strongest
Unbreaking spells like a cornfield trampled under
Elephant's feet.
Today, untimely, I've transgressed the shore

I am in my period
I am the primordial mother earth
It took me so long to realise
One who looked like a guest
Was really a sandal stick
That which seemed like a guest-house
Was really an white ant-hill.
One who had all along been appearing as Kunti
Was really a coiled serpent
Which rises with the touch of a stick.

Come, Oh, the loneliness of the afternoon
The darkness of the moonlit night
The fading light of the setting sun
The fading darkness of the rising sun
Oh! The Lord of the lotus
One who wears the void
Come here...
Come here...
Come here...

## 2

*(The union of the Sun and Kunti and the abandonment of the new-born in the river by Kunti)*

Soon in dense darkness
Was dissolved the past, present and the future
And under the fading cloud
The brown-mole on the nose
Of the naughtiest fairy got swollen
In sheer jealousy
*Yaksha, Raksha, Gandharb, Kinnar, Surasura...*
All closed their eyes

Birds in their nests lay quiet
Tides in the sea rose and remained still, without stir
And from the great void dropped
A pair of gold ear-ring and an armour
Beyond the knowledge of Time.

While arranging
The displaced sari
From the thickness of the leaves
A bird twittered
The night was over
While tying up the loosened hair
The last star in the sky heard
The sound of quick footsteps of someone
Hurrying back from the eroded river bank
Towards the palace!

## 3

My fate had already made
A wooden-chest for me
Before I was born
While floating down the river towards an unending future
Of a horizon that was nowhere in sight
Once had I glanced at my mother
With my twinkling innocent eyes.

In a moment
How remote had she been
It's unfortunate!
Her eyes had become the early morning's dew
On the black-leaves
Of *Katha Tarata* plant

Her forehead
Like the distraught horizon
In the red sorrows of the setting Sun,
The palpitation was
Like the flashes of lightning
From the feathers of the flying cranes
Deep down in the dark clouds
In the last void
Of the moonless sky
Like a tiny twinkling star
My mother then far away from me.

From the womb of an unmarried mother
(Like a fresh Jasmine dropped down
In the gentle breeze)
From ages after ages
For all those millions and millions of unfortunates
Who are born and who are yet unborn,
I am the poor representative,
Me alone…(?)

## 4

The river Ganga
Gradually drifted me away
From my mother
Standing at the bank
Like a stormy night
To my future,
Destined to shape me in another form
Pushed me in another direction
My fate was like a wind
That knows not which way it blows.

By then the day had dawned
When midway in the river
Suddenly I woke up from my sleep
And saw no one around
Little above the horizon
Ahead of me
Was placed a lovely red ball
Called father... father
A ray of light came forth
Up to my lips, my forehead...

The base of the chest felt warm this time
Like my mother's lap
In the mid-air,
I am that poor, orphaned future
Of the unhappy bird who flew away
Laying eggs in a wrong nest,
Below me the river and poisonous snakes
And up above
The hawk hovering in the open sky.

## 5

Would you take *Hilsa*, Madam?
Very tasty *Hilsa*
Along the village path
The regular dry-fish seller- *Kata Ma*
goes with her loud cries
Sometimes
Wearing loom-woven napkin,
Carrying glass-bangles, vermilion
And tuft of peacock feathers on a bamboo lath
Comes Anadi the wandering *Kela*
To the locality

Like festive days.
Childhood passes
Along the village path.
Birds fly back to their nests in the evening,
The crows, myna and the sparrows…
Years come, years go by.

While teasing gently
Mother would get vexed up and say :
"Just get off my lap,
Are you my son?
You, child of an outcaste
I have picked you only
From a river slop…"

Taking my face aside from her breast
I would look at mother's eyes just once
She was silent, with a sullen face
And I do look at the aunts
And elders, standing apart,
A kind of smile hanging from their lips,
A hint of my misfortune,
Saying 'yes', as it were.

Is it only a casual talk,
Or a bolt from the blue?
Echoes the jumping calf
'A child of an outcaste
Are you mine?'
The bird flies in the sky, echoing it:
'A child of an outcaste
Are you mine?'
Casting only a glance
The lizard on the wall draws back

The black-faced male-cricket slips into the drain
Kicking away my lace-toy
I soon hide under the cot.

Just a word
As if that was an unending rain
Of a poor village
And I, myself
A disordered wheel of a bullock cart
Leaning against a wall
Of some dilapidated palace
That is seldom seen.

## 6

I feel sometimes as if
This sands-house I've built
From the dust along the path is not mine…
The hands that leisurely arrange my unkempt hair
Are not that of my mother!
Under conceit and inattention
The eyes become red
As eyes of an eel
Oh, friend!
The river dries up
But not the tears in eyes.

Twisting the button-less wearing
With a *gamchha* tightened
Around the waist
I rush to the grain-yard
Where my father is all attention
Repairing the broken axle.

With love and fear
I do ask him with quivering lips
Father! Mama says
I am a son of an outcaste
And that you picked me from the river bank?
Is it tears in my eyes
Or cloud bursts
In *Murga-Naxatra*?
Is it sweat
Or the age-old sea
Rushing forth in silence
In the pores of my skin?

Before I drop to the ground
Like a withered flower
I am plucked from the branches,
To my father's arms
And while getting tender pats on my back
I jump to my mother's lap again
Like a flower from the hands
Of a Jhamu- dancer.

### 7

Which river bank?
Which outcaste woman
Dares to say so?
Father reacts:
Who are these garrulous women?
'…Basu is our son': concludes father.

Mother bares her breast
And places the nipple
In between my sticky, famished lips

As if a spoonful of *Ganga-water*
Offered to a dying one.

The cries of the whole life,
Lest it should end at one go.
I could hardly bear to look at
Either father
Or mother…
Face to the ground I lay
Two drops of warm water
Fell on my bare back
Open to the sky.

Is it water
Or first drop of rain
On the longing lips
Of this Summer, about to end?
Can't look upward,
They might be drops of tears,
Of my mother or father
Instead of water.

## 8

If asked
They halt and look…
But never say anything.

'This defensive armour on my chest
And this ear-ring on my ears
Why are these with me only,
Why not with others?'
If I ask mother

She says, ask father
If I ask father
He says, ask the *Ganga*
They don't have time
To answer such trifles.
Are they all alike
When grown up?

Shona says:
Oh, brother Basu
Your earrings glow like fire
As the jewel on king-cobra's hood in the dark
As if stars shine in unison
At dawn, and in the evening.

Now, I stepped out of the house
Father was at Hastina;
In the other room Shona was asleep
Tucked into mother's belly.
Ah! What a clear moonlit night!
So bright that books could be read
With bare eyes.
It was calm and quiet
A little noise sometimes, here and there.
A bird twitters: 'Be the end, Be the end'.
Do I only hear
Or others hear it too.

We keep walking together
One is me
And the other is my naughty fate.
We do eat together from one plate
And sleep together on one bed
But strange! We never speak to each other.

I asked mother Ganga,
"Why don't others have
Such earrings, such armours?"
*Janhabi* was startled at my question
Softly patting my young tender feet
With her cool palms
She said:
'Dawn breaks!
The sky is tinged with red
Go, my son
I will tell you tomorrow!'

## 9

No sacred thread on my shoulder
So I prepared myself
To bear his heavy curse
Not uttered yet,
The blood was streaming down
From the thigh, like milk
From my mother's breast
Might have flown endlessly
On that day.
First and foremost he was old
Second frail and weak
And then
If I had said ever
'I am not a Brahmin!'
How could my *Gurudev*
Have borne such a severe shock!
This insect freed me
From many a haunting sorrow.

Possibly, this was no insect
It was perhaps the noblest manifestation
Of what I intend to be.

Quite some time passed
In drawing the probable image
Of that impending curse.
Before the curse was pronounced
I asked myself:
'To seek what pleasure
Oh Karna!
Did you take your birth!
Agreed, you were fated to take this birth
Why did you vow to lead
The life of a hero?
Oh, a friendless, helpless traveller
Marching forward!
You do not belong to this earth
Its history built of the rusted-ego of caste and race
It can never be yours.

It's a fact, really!
No one ever paused to ask
'Aren't you that great vower,
That generous donor
That hero who has made a name?'
One and all ask the same question
'Where have you been brought up
In which dynasty
Your daring defiance
Your sense of self-respect
The concept of your future was nurtured?'
But, Alas!

Is one's birth, one's caste
And one's ancestral lineage
In one's hand?

In assemblies and associations
In *Swayamvara*
And at the battle fields
Why are they eager to know the undesirable history of life
That is ever controlled by the Almighty?
Then, why is the golden flying tail
Of virile manhood
Scorched by a blunt spear?
But there is no answer,
Only the echo comes back
I am the question,
And I am its only answer.

## 10

Have no fear, Oh *Gurudev*
The pupil of *Parsuram*
Shall never ask for the return
Of his fleeting mortal body…
For the precious head of his dearest enemy
He would be dying for ever
Even after his death.

I implore you now to take back
This unsolicited charity, your *Brahmastra*
If that insect had not been the instrument
To reveal that I am *Shudra*, by caste
If you had not inflicted on me
Under the cover of a mere *Brahamastra*

Would not all the valour and virility
Of this poor charioteer's son have ended?
Take back your *Pashupata*
That looks so pale
Denied by my exorbitant self-confidence.
My lofty soul melts
In the heat of your compassion
Let all the ghastliness
Of your previous births
Be bold today.

I shall obey and accept
Whatever you offer
Conviction or condonation.
But do not humiliate
Even for a moment
This non-Brahmin, this unmitigated *Shudra*
And do not degrade
Even for a moment
The disgrace itself.

## 11

Before me lies
The curses and arrows
And, at my back there lies
*Barunabanta,*
A small Drona, made of clay,
A shabby wrestling house
Of sham aristocracy…
Buried under jealousy and distress
Lies the lucid spells of the vedas
And the raised thirsty axe

To strike a strand of pale sacred-thread
Of a decadent Brahmin.
Alas! The most blessed descendant
Of *Bhrugu* is reduced today...

How soon did disappear in a moment
The assurance of safety,
The unfaded deerskin
The holy-stick of *Palasha*
The shining jug
The dazzling axe, the quiver
A thin stream of water
In the middle of a corn-field.
After harvesting is over,
The play house of dragonfly, butterfly and squirrels !
How did they all vanish :
The shadow-shaded cool leaf-cottage,
Filled with fragrance of incense-sticks
Off my master
In whom is manifested
The story of the Sun !

Now the time for the dreaded curse drew nearer
The sound of footsteps of which new comer
Do I hear in the veins
Along the blood-streams!
Who showered on me
The faded leaves,
Of felled *Saragi-tree,*
From above !

Oh, *Gurudev* !
I am not deceitful,
A bewildered son of a charioteer

That has no past nor future,
I am a *Shudra*.
Have just extended my hands to faith alone
That has eluded my reach.
An aimless passer-by
I have sometimes asked the pretence
About the painful history
To survive and live somehow.
On the verge of death I have begged for a palmful of water
To the mirage by mistake.
I am the charioteer,
The mover of the helpless.
Lo and behold,
How I have stilled
The dance of eternity !

## 12

How can I cross
Such a long fence of pleasure?

If any god or monk in disguise
Have set out late,
Come, I am waiting.
Take away the excess of my happiness
To prepare some kisses
Some sulking *Bisikeshan* badly needs,
For the chest of an unarmed enemy
That craves for
Some more hearty hugs.

Oh! naughty paramour
Of my pleasure!

If no one needs
Then move aside,
From the narrow cow-path of my future
Running through the harvested field.
I have to sit today
On the vacant culvert
At the end of my village
Looking at the twinkling stars
From behind the clouds.
I am to listen today to my lullaby
Forgotten in the distant ragi field
With all my heart.

## 13

They too enquired
About my caste and clan
My father's identity
'Caste, oh…caste!'
My heart
Not tied by mother's milk
Rent in two
In anger and hatred.
My face got red
Like a midday sun
(In shame or in anguish?)
I said: caste?
My caste is the glory
I have earned with my arms.

And said: Just listen
Oh! You fellows, proud of your caste
Sitting cozily
Under the golden umbrella!

Don't you feel ashamed
Asking a man about his caste,
So late, in so much of light,
And in such a loud voice
That is audible to all?
Yes, I am the son of a charioteer
But if you have real courage, tell me
Who is the father of this *Partha*,
The son of *Kunti*
Born in the noble dynasty of *Bharat*
Sure enough, I am the son of a charioteer.

Under the foot-wear of yours
Made of sandalwood
Being a rare oblational-offer to the Guru
I had startled your heart on another day
I am that blood-drenched severed finger…
Again you are asking about the caste?
In reply, just see
How my hands clench into fist
And how it keeps swelling,
This war-hungry chest of mine!

This time
They changed the mode of question
Enquired about the dynasty
Looked for flaws in attire
The royal umbrella, the crown
And keenly observed the oscillating *Chamara*
I might have just melted into the ground
Without any distinct identity in my favour
If someone would not have
Patted his fearless hand

On my helpless shivering shoulder.
I just hated myself for keeping quiet.
Before anyone came forward to give me shelter
Why didn't I say point-blank
On their face, those idiots
With this simplest answer…
"It's not so easy to trace out
The source of a hero or a river
Maybe, the only root of a hero
Is this bow and arrow…"

While my fate was out to bury me
Under the heap of those dry leaves
Who rushed forward to crown me
With this invaluable diadem?
For a disowned, nondescript neglect
Who was this supremely merciful being
Carved on this orphan's forehead
'The king of *Anga*'.

The first ever public acceptance
Of a distressed and the downtrodden
A poor charioteer's son that I am,
Don't know how I shall ever pay back
Such a heavy-debt!!

## 14

Or if,
I had honestly told my name,
The name by which I am known
In the village
And in the slum-habitation,

The sun would have forgotten
It's time to rise
Out of shame and humiliation.


The little lotus-bud, in the distant village pond
Would have stopped midway while blooming
The small grains of rice
Broken, pecked by birds
Would have remained as such and dropped
In the mid-field.
A million of Gandhis
And thousands of Sessans would have gone back
Without being born.
Then what was the right answer
To the questions put by the people?
What might be my real name
My identity acceptable to the society?

I am the holiest and the glorious sin
Of all the maiden-mothers
Covered under the river-sands
In the poor, empty shell of the oyster
With a desire to create
I am that drop of rain under the *Swati star*,
The earliest beginning of all beginnings
Whether I am born or not born
I am the everlasting red vacuum
In every womb forever.

## 15

I have ever been the first-born

The hum and the murmur, not audible to others
The solitary lullaby
And all the love for the childhood,
I only have touched the earth first
I am the first born always, down the ages.

Before all the bangles and vermilion came their way
I am the ornament
That the girls wear…
I am the unmarried sigh, ending in death
Of all those married women
For those who hold all the meanings
Of life as meaningless
I am the means for living
The name of all the unwanted
All the undesired in this world
I am that *Radheya*
The son of the Sun-god.

What may be my real name?
A fitting identity
Acceptable to the society!

I am the deceit of the deprived
Shame of the ashamed
Defeat of the defeated
And the flag of the broken chariot…

## 16

It is not that-
No one ever asks me – 'who am I?'
The pedlar that returns with his back to the palm-tree
That touches the horizon,
The old man lying on the torn mat
Who counts his last remaining days
Looking at the lonely first star of the evening,
The barren mango branch in the village grove
That has stopped blooming since long
Asks sometimes 'who are you?'

The bird whose young innocents are dead earlier
Have been swallowed up by the snake
The crest of the wedding-crown
Of the bride who died a premature death,
Sparkling in the moonlit sea-water
Sometimes asks 'Who are you?'

The same question echoes back
From the quiet blue hill – 'Who are you?'
The half-seen, half-hidden stream
Repeats the refrain – 'Who are you?'
While climbing the tree
The squirrel stops, looks back
Unable to decide the strange from the familiar
The galaxy of seven stars
In the endless void, and the whole universe itself
Stands before me, a question itself.

The unending fate of those unfortunates
Who can neither live nor die

I answer:
And I, a poor drowsy me,
Caught in the sun rays
Streaming into the room
Through a hole in the thatched roof
A foolish word
That escaped the unwary lips
And finds no way to come back
Unrest at mines or Agro-lands,
A sacrificial post,
The men at the head of the long queues
In front of temples, mosques
Answer…

If anyone had asked
My real, unambiguous name
What would have been the answer?
If I had revealed my real identity
What would have happened
To this world on that day?
What would have happened
To the fate
Of my dearest enemy Arjuna ??

## 17
*(Context: The Swayamvar of Draupadi…)*

Now, they looked at one another
Basudeva at Drupada
Drupada at Dhrishtadyumna
And Dhrustadyumna at Panchali
At this time
The dialogue that had been memorised

But forgotten was heard
From the hesitant garland:
"Oh, you
So called son of a charioteer!
Withdraw your bow
In this groom-choosing ceremony
Of a noble bride
How irrelevant it looks, the presence of Karna."

Now, who is that competitor
A Non-Kshatriya
At the end of the long line of Kshatriyas?
'A substitute of Karna
This Brahmin, who is he?
'Much stronger objection'
But why do *Krishna's* lips
Suffer in silence, Oh you friends?

Is it just a formality
Of a marriage already solemnised?
Am I the only person to win defeats
Of all the wars?
Oh, the precious reprimand
Of my misfortune!
Did you not get any ordinary lips
To utter, and you held up in exchange
My only tender love?
And turned the flower to the spark of fire,
And the butterfly, to a mere insect.

How much conspiracy is scared of
The pride and bravery
I understood

As it came hiding its name
At the moment of aiming
In the lakh shooting.
The raised hands of Panchali remained static
Turning my neck I sneered:
'Are you mad or what,
Who shot the arrow
And whom do you garland??'

## 18

*(Karna returns from the ceremony of Swayamvar not being accepted due to his lowly family background. There is a river on the way. An old banyan tree stands at the bank. A little ahead, the marching troops. Exhausted, Karna sits in the shadow of the tree, unmindful.)*

Before sticking in your hair (not of yours!)
The half-bloomed marigold
How did it fade and drop?
When I tried to reach out to your cheeks (not of yours!)
To wipe the tears
The redness (of chewed betel leaves) of whose lips
Spilled on my palm…!

The crow took away my collyrium-case
And the unknown bird my rest
The brown kite flew away with my bed
And the rat ran off with all my pleasures.

I am a bare foot-hedge
Of a faded lee-dye
A forehead of decayed sandals,
The palanquine refused me a place in it

The garland grew obstinate
(Play-chest of which player, I wonder
The dawn of which night?)

The light laughs at me during day
And the shadow in the evening
My own voice seems vague and strange
(Oh *Radheya*!)
How long can I seal my year…?

The path asks me my father's name
The sky enquires about my address…
The labour room at *Mushaphirkhana*
Where a fire was kept aflame to keep me warm
And a vulture suckled me.

The slate has cursed me
And the chalk seeks to know my caste
I am the darkness…
And, the scoldings incarnate
I'm the desert that gleams still
At the end of my long walk.

I promised to offer my defensive-armour
And also the ear-rings of mine
I promised
To be the faded lily,
In the play-dice of orphaned kids…
Leave those who took a different track
Those who are nearby, tell me
If it would turn to tears
The rest of the outcries of the earth
And flow down from my eyes!

I am the battle and the battle-ground myself
I do shoot my own arrow at myself
I win and then lose myself
I die and then I cry for myself.

I do weep and wipe my own tears
I do withdraw, and pat my back
I am the river...
And I do flow on, eroding my bank,
In a few moments I am torn,
I am the straw-mat in a small house
I am the wood
And also the wood-pecker.

I am the full-moon of the distant horizon
And the darkness of the sea nearby
I went as a handkerchief
And was reduced to
( Say, how and why)
A scarf, covering the corpse !

## 19

*[Context: To collect revenue for Rajasuya Yajna the Pandavas' mobilisation of troops and attack of Bhima on Champa Nagari. After a day's fight, at the behest of Kauravas, Karna makes a treaty. On the next morning of war Karna's water oblation and thereafter, prayer of a woman to get back her son killed in war.]*

Karna asked after oblation in water –
Is there anyone at the bank, praying for something
Yes, Oh Angaraj, here is one
Can you offer what she wishes for?
Ask me not for my Dharma,

Not my virility and chivalry
Other than these in Karna's life
Nothing is there that cannot be offered.
Setting the fire of war, you reached a truce later
In exchange for the State's revenue.
Give me back my son
Whose life was lost in the war
Fated to be undecided.

Vain is that war
That leads to neither a win nor a loss
Do you have the right
To send my son
To such a fight?

I am dying already, oh mother
Kill me not
With your words, more dreadful than the thunder.
The King of Champanagar
Will be the apple of your eye
In the small cottage of yours
From tomorrow onwards.
You sprinkle salt on the wound
That is yet to heal.
Oh! Deceitful Karna, do you think
A mother who has lost her son doesn't know
What is pure and what is fake?

These words are not fake, Oh mother
They lie indelible, carved on a rock
The golden crown of Champanagari
Will adorn some other's head, tomorrow.
Being the shelter of million sons,

Do not take such a terrible vow
For I have learnt now how   to bear
The grief and agony of losing millions of sons.

## 20

*[ During the Rajasuya Yajna of Jujhesthi all on a sudden, noticing Kunti]*

Why this lady is not then
Like other women?
Whether I sit or stand
She looks at me as if she sees me
For the first time.
She looks at me
But the moment our eyes meet
As fast as lightning
She looks the other way
As if she has not seen me at all.

I feel like asking so often
But I fail to do so
Out and out my complete replica
Who is this woman?
Is she the woman
Who like a thief has stolen the gold mohur coin
And has left the empty vessel lying on the floor
And me, like the gold mohur
Unable to come back to the vessel
Live harassed me all my life.

Striking her head on the chest
Of a monk, ill-tempered and obstinate,
Yesterday in the afternoon,

Her lamenting voice I heard in my dream
As if it encircled my tomb of my previous births
At some forgotten places.
She is unlike any other woman
Since I was afraid of the crow and *Kakomina*
In my childhood
But, since the day I saw her, I'm afraid of myself
This star, this moon
This river, this lake
They all might say:
"This house is not mine
This father is not my father
This land is not my land."

Or they might not say:
This *Radhi ma* is not my mother
Trying to say a thousand times
I finally remained quiet
Such a striking resemblance
Such similar features
Am I Karna
Or someone else is?

## 21

*( Basu at the guest house of Indraprastha. Remembrance of boyhood love…)*

I dreamt today
A marvellous palace
A garden attached to it and beyond the garden
A deserted stable…
At other part of the garden
A copper-coloured teenage boy

Ties the loose hair
Of a girl of angelic beauty.
They sweat in profusion
In contentment, in fear.
Their faces fresh
In a moment
And stale in another.

I strained my ear
As the girl whispered
" Oh! My first love
My friends may tease me
'What happened – How did it happen…'
Wipe the chewed betel-leaf mark off my cheek
Mother would heckle me with queries
'What happened, How so…'
With you please, trace out for me
The anklet's-ball!"

Ah! This afternoon
With its blend of honey
And Koil's haunting melody
You the hottest sun, Oh the *Ear-born*!
And I am the water underneath !!

After it…
The bangles' sound was heard from the stars
Oh, learned!
The sleep was disturbed
That palace and the garden
That stable and the hero of the dream
Remained unknown as before
Though they looked familiar
Oh, learned!

## 22

While going alone on a deserted road
With birds nowhere in sight
Like small mangoes and buds
Beating against the southern-wind
( In an orchard of some remote village...)
Poured into my memory
The lonely-crowd of your maiden-smile.

Ah! How desirable was the sweet pain
When you crossed my path
And seeing me as if you didn't see me at all
You would turn aside quickly and walk along
Like a herd of hungry children
Running after sandy-sweet bananas
Like the poorest beggar
Eager to collect coins thrown along the path
In a funeral procession.

How many lost kites, swinging in your sky...
Mementos of my enemies' love for you.
I, a poor boy from the fisherman's slum
At the outskirt of the city
Is it written on my forehead
By some intolerant God
To stay like this, casting shameless glances.

Sometimes I am seized with a longing
For those ecstatic engrossed hours and days
Of our early youth
Those carefree days
Of those vacant, no-work days at *Gurukul*
When flowers and leaves from the nearby *Shirish* tree

Like little mischiefs would just come flying,
And touch the ground
Only after caressing your dishevelled hair
And rosy cheeks…

And I would snatch the spear-grass
From your frock with floral design
And you would thrust
Into my hand pickle prepared by your mother,
Just about to speak, our lips would forget
The words that were to be spoken.

## 23

Sometimes I wish
You would be rolling down
From the tip of the knitting-needle
As a stream of blood
Into my heart in deep silence
And I would be taking you
In a canoe of a lonely shore
Into the dreams of the depth of a lake
Through the dense mist
Where the trees and hills at the bank are not visible.

Your shy self shall form the sunset
Night by the darkness of your hair
The lone-star's dawn shall be formed
Out of your timid twinkling light

So also I hope sometimes
To lead you to the interior
Of a remote deserted moss-walled temple

And say:
" For once be an idol
Devoid of cloth and decors
For once you become
The long moonlit night
And get into every pore of my being
I, the fallen sperm
Of an artist in exile
And a drained empty water-lily…"

But, Alas!
Nothing happens my way as I desire
Time halts
As a wall-clock, out of order
And unrepaired.

## 24
*(Karna had just returned from the Rajasuya Yajna of the Pandavas, a million thoughts on his mind, with no scarf on the shoulder. A sense of unwantedness arose in his wife Brushali from deep within.)*

'Where did you leave your scarf, dear
At which harem ?
Brushali's mild protest
In a soft tender voice
Resting her face on my back:
I stood at the edge of the window,
My eyes fixed on the sky, with countless stars.

Turning around
I held in my palms
Brusha's face, sad and sullen

And I said:
"For a while
Just one word 'gymnasium'
Came to your lips
But these days I find
You say 'harem' every now and then
Oh tell me, what's the matter?
Who may be that fortunate lady
Whom that harem
Of your doubts mean?"

While playing her fingers
Through hairs on the chest
Brusha said:
'Why, what about your Panchali!'
'My Panchali, in whose dictionary
Karna stands for hatred, only hatred?'
'Yes, your Panchali, in whose dictionary
Karna connotes love, only love.'

Before disintegrating into pieces
Gathering myself intact
I said: Brusha!
The last game of dice
made out of the bones of Jarasandha,
Might end in futility by my utterances
The hands that sent me down to Ganga
Have their selfish goals.
The hands that appeared from nowhere
In the gymnasium and placed a crown on me
Are selfish too.
Brusha ! Where is friendship
Where is that love, deemed to be eternal!

In an effort to make me stable
Leaning her body against mine
Said Brusha:
'Then, tell me oh! my love
While I sat one day among my friends,
Patting the ear-base of my son
Why did she remark-
Like father, like son
But where is his *Kundal*?

Looking at your reflection once
In the water-pool at Indraprastha
Why did she whisper into her companion's ears
'Friend,
Twelve months in a year
It could have been equally divisible by six
If he had been my husband'.

## 25
*(Episode: Duryodhan argues in support of the game of dice. Karna wavers)*

I looked at the sky
Covered by
A piece of dark cloud
As mysterious as the story of my birth,
A grey crane was flying across
Touching that cloud
My lonely heavy sigh as it were

All on a sudden
The blank surroundings laughed out
Like my treacherous fate

And in that laughter was heard
The voice of Duryodhan:
" Friend, you get annoyed
Hearing the name of dice,
But isn't war itself a game of dice?
Whether it's known or not,
The power of enemy
One has to jump into the fray
Whether it's rightly judged or not,
The weaponry of enemy
One does get into the turmoil
Whether the outcome is a victory or defeat
One has to fix the arrow in the bow.
Oh friend!
Isn't war itself a game of dice?

Not dice?, not dice?
The words echoed:
All the flower branches in the garden were stunned
And so were the hillocks, my confidence too
Earned since my childhood.

Before the last echo was resisted
From the glass carvings on the pillar
The voice of my reflection was heard:
"Karna! You hate the game of dice too much
You fear it a lot, isn't it?
But, then what is dice
And what is not?
Was that not a gamble of motherhood
To set you floating in the river
In your orphaned state?
This smile, this sulk

Isn't this conjugal life a gamble?
This play
This calamity
Isn't this friendship with its fun and hostility
A game of dice?
Oh, Karna! You are not inclined to this game, isn't it?

'Oh, Karna, isn't it, Oh Karna, isn't it!'
The echo resounded…
The stars in the space were excited
Meteor dropped in the far-off field
Jackal howled and the owl hooted.

I felt helpless and thought:
The unbroken loyalty to husband of my Brushali,
As holy as the fire of Yajna
The simple, frank, unpretending
Nature of my Brushaketu,
As transparent as the dews of dawn,
The pure love
Of my *Radhi bou*
Like a burning wick
That has remained unextinguished
Against the wind
The ascetic prayer of my *Adhi Baba*
Like the evening in a village after storm
And above all,
While floating helpless in the depth of the river
How like a piece of straw
The friendship that Hastina offered came my way,
Are all these like games of dice, like gambling?

## 26
*(Disrobing of Draupadi. And invocation of Karna to her)*

In the beginning, that piercing sound
One hears in the quiet of the night
Later a mild and soon after
The sound of flute full of ecstasy
Then a harmonious divine music
Sometime the lilt of Veena
And some other time the rapid *Dunduvi*...
From where does it come,
Not easy to trace.

There appeared a flash of shining light
Through the canopy
Flourished in length and, little by little,
Touched your body.
Then, the tune of flute, got sharper
Laden with fear and anger
The desperate and beastly Dusha's laughter
Sounded cruel and loathsome
By and by.

Your closed hands remained steady and still
Without any exertion
And in your hands was a line of
Bewailing prayer
Like an innocent dragonfly fluttering
In the arum-leaf of your infancy.
Closed weepy eyelids
Like a calmness in the countryside
At the break of dawn...

Endless sarees of varied colours
Were sewn as though to your twist of wearings
That touched your naval
Blue, deep-blue, green, red, violet, orange, yellow and so on…
Ah! The mighty-hands
Of the second Kourava
Looked like the mandible of a black-ant
Dragging grains of sugar.

Now the blowing of conch
That was to be heard
Before the beginning of war, was heard…
A dreadful river of blood
From the mountain of sarees, rushed forth
A million severed heads
Bloomed in it like lilies
The babble of babies
The humming of bees,
The song of birds wobbled in it
And there was no space left.

I looked at your bluish feet
That touched your yellow-silken cloth
And closed my eyes…
And said :
"*Krishnaa* !
You are my love, and my dislike
You are my downfall and my ascent you are
You are my reprimand and my glory
You are my moonlessness
And my full moon night too
You are my arrow in the quiver

My battlefield you are
You make me live
And you only cause my death.

I bow before you, oh tear-eyed
I pray you the Divine, with hair dishevelled
I bow before you, oh my supreme shelter
I pray you, clothed in celestial yellow...!!

## 27

On that day I saw, not you Panchali
I witnessed before me
The helplessness itself
No lac-dye on the foot
No *kumkum* on the forehead
The tresses clutched in another's hand
A one-piece of cloth draped round you
On that day
I saw, not you Panchali !
But the helplessness itself stood in visible form.

Does helplessness also hate
A charioteer's son?
Is he not a man like you
Or like others ?
Tell me... Panchali !

Spinning and spinning like a top
When you became still and quiet before me
Looked up, raising your eyelids
I thought things would happen perhaps like this
And you would say:

'Oh! *Angaraj*!
Never mind those past deeds
Whatever I said then, losing my wits
That day at Kampilya
Forget that…
That time the issue was offering my garland
To choose my groom
But today, it's my womanhood
Then it was the eyes of the moving fish
Today it lies unmoved.

Then was the deceitful object to win over
Today it's a real one
Then it was one lakh kings but for one
Today it's you alone
Oh, my dearest
Now, accomplish this precious me you aimed at.

## 28

Now things will happen this way
By my unsheathed-sword
A hairy ugly hand that clutches your hair
Shall be dismembered.
Like the endless rain in *Mruga Nakshatra*
The arrows of mine
Would make them flee,
The dumb courtiers
Along with your husbands…

This time I would get down in darkness
On the only road of my destiny

That ends at Champa Nagar.
No other single sound would be heard
From anywhere in this land
Except for the rustle
Of rearranging your saree.

Then...
Your choking voice will be heard in sleep :
'Karna !
How obstinate are you !
You just came back
And asked for nothing in return...
Did you fear ?
That I might invite you
To the first night of my marriage
Where in the dim light of the lamp
Would be seen
The vacant seat meant for you.

## 29

Did I ever desire so
That they would hold you by your hair
And drag you out of the kitchen
And disrobe you in the court
While I was alive.

Before raising your hands up
I was your not-yet-finished
*Non-Arjun* love
I was yet the half-prayer
Of all your distress.
Whether you accept it or not

I would have covered
Every inch of your disgrace
By every moment of the rest of my life
If the cruel opponent of our love
Had not been either Krishna or Arjuna
Could I remain inert at all
While I breathed ?

I know
At the behest of your father(?),
Ascertained earlier,
You have shared yourself
In turns
In the blood of each husband of yours
You have shared yourself
In the cloud, in the peacock's dance
And in the tune of flute
Played at midnight hours !!

Is there any open way
For me to get you
Except your ruin and wreckage?

A ruined lover I am
What more may be my last victory
Except a war with myself
Bloodshed of my own
And my own defeat?

## 30

*(Place : Dwaita forest: Context : the Ghosha yatra)*

The flag
Made of the wavy hair,
The war-cry bursting out of the eyebrows
The jingling anklet and the ornament at the waist
Would have been the war-drum
The captivating weapon made from
The graceful dance and smiles
And the glances like binding ropes...

Such a battle-field was beyond
What one could imagine.

Like a cannon ready to fire
From behind a moat encircling an old fort
The bluish nipple would be peeping
Through the drenched cloth...
The half-bathed
Celestial maiden-musicians,
Thousands of earthly maid-servants
Binding the veils at the waist
Ready to bathe
With the ordinary unmatching language
On their lips
May be gathering at the other bank...

In the middle
There would be the *Dwaita Bana*
With its pond of limpid water
And the lotus-buds
Surrounded by the black-bees flitting about

At one side of the pond was Chitrasen,
Turban on head, dressed in golden-dhoti,
Drums in hand...
Stands Duryodhan
With bow and arrows,
A battle terror
At the other bank...
Out of imagination
Was such a battlefield.

Is it a battle-field
Or theatre pendal?
Rising from behind the intermediate space
It ends there
A note of ecstatic music...
Neither Drona nor Parasuram said
That even jingling of an Anklet-ball
May at times devastate
The whole of Hastina...?

How wonderful it is to find
This bow of *palasha* joined
By this arrow of *Abira*...!
Neither I nor my companion
Oh God !
Who has learnt this *Gandharva Astra*...!

Who has studded all the stars
In the dishevelled hair of the woman
Who has made this air so intoxicating
With all the sandals of the forest?
Who is sending these heart-aches so frequently
Like an embrace...

Ah! In between the gap of the breasts
Of a mere amorous woman
Is imprisoned my *Managobinda*
The *Bharat barsha* of tomorrow !

Rotten leaves lie all around
Where is the battlefield
Where is my distracted chariot?
You term it as an escape on my part
As my defeat...?
Can there ever be a battle-field for Karna
Where there is no Arjuna ?

## 31

On that day
A splendour of new fresh cloud
Appealed to me
For my ear-rings and my defensive-armour
(I was saying my prayers)
Opening my eyes
I looked once at the sun, the omnipotent
And once at the mother earth
And laughing to myself thought :
If a father would not do
This much for a son,
Who else would do ?
( I wished I had such a father with teeth
To gnaw and suck a thorn from the foot ?)
Thought : Shall I give or not...!

Just at this time
From the place beyond Kurukshetra

Came to my view
A weepy, teary face...
The vermilion on the parting of her head
Looked brighter and more red
Than my heart and vanity...
The lac-day on her feet
Seemed more humble
Than the helpless innocence of my mother...
The bangles on her hand
Sounded to me like the first offer of love
Of a woman
Most desired and craved for.

From a height
Beyond the range of my eyes
The peacock-tuft of eternity
Of the endless time
And an illusory evening of some afternoon
It looked as if
The uncertain vermilion
Of my bluish-tender-love
( From the blessed forehead)
Is being washed away in the blood
Of my dear enemy ( wasn't he Arjuna?)
I felt as if
The arrow aimed at me,
Not of my enemy,
Is breaking down into pieces
The bangles, one by one
Of *aguru* scented hands of my beloved.

## 32

Beloved is beloved
She may be the wife of my enemy
Or betrothed to my closest friend
She may be the distant-star
Or a tuft of sacred grass at hand...

I shall wipe out all her tears
Her helplessness
Offering every bit of my life-span
I will raze to the ground all my stubbornness
Made out of the ignorance of the world...

Arjun is my enemy,
And this is the least reason:
We both fight the same battle
Being in two opponent groups...
Arjun is my enemy,
Since we are in love
With the same girl
(Love or illusion of love?)

This time I looked up with open eyes
At the illusory cloud
Rising forward
From the *Mamu Bhanaja* corner of my death,
And settled now
On the fragrant tender mango-branch
Of my future.
I said : I shall offer one
Either the death of Arjun or that of mine
I commit.

Except the love of that woman
With her knee-long hand
And her long flowing hair
And her body of bluish colour
I can give all that I have with me
Including my victory.
( What is that mere ear-ring and defensive armour in her presence)
Looking at the water of oblation today
Oh! my miserly Brahmin !
I commit.

## 33

I have heard
From the whispers
Of the winter sun-rays :
That I do have
An unwritten horoscope
Of my distressed birth...,
Now you read out
Every bit of it
You turn and twist the flow of time,
*Dark- tamal*, my
Time-eternal.

But, I am not all mine any more
Setting aside
The illusion of the royal-turban,
Royal umbrella and fly-brush
Have climbed down
From the clan, the family-lineage and glory,
And have skilfully escaped

From the ill-conceived womb of my fate.

My moderate talk
As brief and light as the afternoon naps
Tell me now :
"Karna!
Under the soot of history
You do suffer like distressed
Elephants, horses, drums, flags;
Your jewel-studded wisdom?

You held both my arms
Straightened the bent-down face
And said :
" You are only your own intimate identity
Promise is your bow and arrow
Life, the battle,"

You offered a rebel's collyrium
To my dull languid eyes
And brightness to the pale physique
Oh, Keshaba !

Things that I had presumed
As noble descent and pedigree so long
Are indeed I realise today
Are the shackles that impede
My glory and prosperity...
Not the defensive armour
Nor the ear-rings;
These are the mountains
Where sets my sweat, my blood and my virility
And my sinking fortune.

In my sleep and in my waking
I see today only one person
Who opened the eyelid of the fallen
The protector of the pauper
The undeclared monarch of the destitute
The visionary Duryodhan
The son of the Blind !
He is the sight, he is vision
He is the mouth, spell, nose and breath.
He is my ultimate faith that is left in me
He is my horizons, below and above
In all the ten directions.
He is my purple-red desire
That goes a step ahead and turns back.

## 34

His turn is over
And now it is mine…
He is the supreme
My companion, my bosom friend !

Branch of the tree overhead,
Impenetrable darkness
Beneath is the lion with a human body
You are the pretence, you the deceit…
Should I push down at your behest
To blood and tears
To death and defeat
My managobinda who has fallen asleep?
I am the food of the starving
Identity of the strange and unknown
Honour of the insulted

Rescue of the repressed
A drop of sweat
Softly moving
On one's exhausted forehead,
I am Karna...

You are the sea !
A deep-dark pretension
Moving away farther
With each step
You are an indistinct prayer
Curling up towards the sky
From the depth of the Ganga
Like the smoke from the cooking place of destitutes.
I am Karna,
A lonely crane
Absorbed in its own sorrows and remorse.
In the middle of a dark remote corn-field
In the evening of *Bhadrav*...
You are the approaching darkness,
Time eternal,
The limitless vastness of the void.

## 35

Oh! The supreme fisherman !
Withdraw your magical fishing net
A short-lived fish I am
Weak
Bearing on my back all the humiliations
Of the destitutes.
Walking nameless for hundreds of years
A nameless weary traveller

Struck down by the sun
*Sujodhan* is my banyan-root.

He is the shore
The sea of an invisible-end
Remaining part of humiliation of my defeats!
Let it be like that
Pull not the rope
I have not yet repaid
Even a small bit of Hastina's endless debt!

Ever absolute
Oh, *Sudarshan*!
If you will keep or not
This little prayer
Of the incompleteness.
Not a treaty,
I beg a battle rather.
I'm Karna,
Born of the human feet,
A long desert of
A thousand ungranted wishes,
A blank space of
A thousand unfulfilled rights.

( A little pity if have on this poor miserable)
From the North-west corner
Of my uncertain fate
You come down
The battle field of magical-cloud
Smeared with ashes
Oh, *Dambarudhar*!
My ultimate burial ground
Say 'let war take place…'

## 36

Oh! Keshab !
I too remember sometimes
The happenings of the bygone days
Some heart-aches
Some tears the bed absorbs
And the lips suck some more
As no one is there to wipe them off.

The sun also said the same thing
That they tell me today
But, after the river has flown down
Does it ever go back to the mountain again?
Once the rain-drops fall
Do they go back to the cloud again?

In the midnight hours
I don't know why
I get up all on a sudden
The dreams dreamt already,
Like *light clear* cloud
Of the night on *Kuanrpunei*
Float before me again
And I see, You hold the crown on my head
With your *tamal*-like blue hands
Bhima wears
Shoes on my feet
Yudhisthira blows the fly-brush
Dhananjaya acts as body-guard
All others at the door !

And also see :

Uttara serves delicious food
With utmost care
Panchali offers
A plain betel
With a pleasant smile.
From a distance is seen
Another rare sight
My orphaned future
Blooms in the still eyes
Of Kunti, my biological mother.

Madhusudan !
Does dream give only that
Which life denies !
It shows the pond,
But gives instead the garland of faded lilies
Offers ruby and pearls
But, gives the raw-brass !!

### 37

Oh, *Dwarakahish*!
Why is my sleep so full of
Strange endless dreams ?

Only last night I saw :
All the houses and villages
Cities and countries
Have turned into a vast burial-ground,
I can only hear
The sounds of footsteps getting fainter
To my ears…
From a distant river-bank

Lullabies are heard
The blanket covering the body
Turning into a desert
And spreading over the whole body
The rivers are returning to the hills,
A broken wheel of a bullock-cart
Is pressing hard on my throat.

A divine lady, garland in hands
Is standing on the horizon
While I try to take a step towards her
She hides herself
In the thin fog…
Every evening the children die
And every morning
The bangles of the last night
Break.

Why such strange dreams
Crowd my sleep endlessly
Oh, Lord of Dwaraka !

My outcry
Woke up Brushali from her sweet slumber
And she said :
"Lord of Dwaraka !
Who do you speak to?
Oh, the master of sleep!"

## 38

'Kunti'
Utter not this name
Even for once
Poor lady
Has turned into a rock
After giving birth
Has forgotten to speak.
Mother of six sons
Is dead, Oh Lord Krishna
One who is alive is the mother of five sons.

Never disclose it Oh, God!
I am telling you
This unspoken episode of that night...
While floating along in a chest
I looked once at the bank
And saw:
Scared of what people would say
And the public disgrace
The poor woman has prepared
Her own pyre alone...
Has set into it the sandalwood of blind aristocracy
Has poured on it the first milk-drop
Of motherhood as ghee
And the pyre is all aflame
Oh, Lord Krishna
The cruel heartless fire of dead-conscience !!

What I saw after that...
My hair-root swells up
Tongue dries up and sticks to the pallet
I saw : Painted with lac-dye and saffron,

Jingling the bangles
A maiden walking out of the pyre
In the darkness of the night
Towards Hastina.

## 39

Who are they really,
Friend or foe?
Sometimes
I ask the fences and walls
And sometimes I ask myself…
Under a cloud-sick sky
I am a mere dragonfly with its feathers plucked
Distressed and full of dust on the road.

A sorrowful water-lily
In the early morning following full moon-night,
I am the dew-drops
Dropping from the sky that has no stars
On the deserted sandy plain
With some shrubs here and there.
And I
Avoiding the eyes of the owner
A distressed tear
Shining on a boy's cheek
At the lonely hotel-slab.

I remember sometimes
Their cruel pitiless faces
Seeking my clan, caste, throne and dynasty
And one who had answered on that day
To those complex, difficult questions.
Though I don't remember
A single answer?

One who had floated a piece of dead-straw,
A piece of assurance on safety
Ahead of this ant being washed away?
Who had held in check
The fire soots of jealousy
Flying towards the heaps of leaves
Of my self-respect
On the wet tuft of straw
Of his brother-hood??

## 40

Who held like an umbrella
Over my unprotected head
A scanty sky of shelter?
Who embraced my icy-cold boyhood
In an warm palm
Like that of a bird's nest?
Who, who gave me a clothful of protection
To cover my naked body
Who placed a piece of earth
Under my tottering feet?

If they are none of mine
Then, who is she to me?
A deceitful family-hood(!)
That has slowly melted like a distant laughter
Near that palm tree
Where gradually this sky ends !!

A born-foolish mother
Trusting the faintly-burning cradle
To the care of vultures

In that lonely night
To remain as a maiden…
Who is she to me?

I am an unwritten line
Of *Devanagari* of that ill-fated one
Left behind
By *Sathi Budhi,*
For the evening never came
Nor the day did dawn.
Who is my friend
Who is my foe??

## 41

Am I baby plant
Of a mistaken-seed
Planted
At the wrong river-bank?
One bank is built of doubts
And I wonder
If the other is in fear?

After many a spring
The flowers did bloom
Some you made the sweet-smelling *Malati*
And some others you made
The fragrant jasmine
But why did you make those flowers
That don't smell good at all
Thus you turned into one lie
Crores of truth.
Why did you make it?

My own leaves drop off
My own branch
In the span of a day I shudder seventeen times
I grow worried
At the sound of my own voice
I am deaf to my own ears
Why do you ask about others
I am unknown to myself
My jingling-bell rings round my neck
But I get scared
As if the bell is of others!!

Some deserted, and some crowded
The tree bears as much fruits as they are plucked
When the bamboo-pole is raised towards it
The sky lowers down
And stretches its hands.
So many ghosts and so many birds
Noisy chirpings sometimes
And utter silence the next moment
Sometimes the hands clap
And laughter resounds
And, some other times my soul flies away
When in water I catch
My shaking shadow.
There's no wood-cutter nor axe
The stroke beats under the root
Ah! What a thunder
Without rain is it ?

Am I the first blood
Of the first-sin

Come near me
I shall make you see
Am I the first letter
Of the first love
Come near me
I shall make you learn !!

## 42

*(Leading the war is yet to materialise.
Karna has a strange dream)*

Whose helpless cry is it
At the outskirt of people's living place
In the dead of night?
The cry drew nearer and nearer
And I saw
An indistinct image of a woman.

Many hills and mountains and rivers
Trees and creepers and chirping of birds
Many a forgotten sunrise and sunset
The garlands of severed heads of soldiers killed in wars
Seemed to have formed her body
And of those getting ready to fight
Hung round her neck
And also her waist
Clothes drenched in blood.
And her hair appeared
As if it would wipe out
All the stars in the sky
In the twinkling of an eye.

There I saw at one place
My play-house made of dusts and sand,
Headless marble toys
Of my childhood days
At one place
Disfigured earthen horses of village goddess
Saw my wedding-crown made of thermocol
Gathered at the shore by sea-tides
The old letters of my beloved
And the usual daily doubts of my wife...
At one place, a familiar crow
And at other my *Radhi Bou*
Returning home
After offering water to the old pipal tree.

A sharp outcry was heard
From the lips of that phantom woman
Clamour and shouts to stop the war
Was heard from the dead.
Also was heard the bragging
Of those alive on the verge of death.

Now I asked
Who are you, Oh Mother
At the outskirt of this country-side
At this lonely place, standing alone
In such late hours of night?
And the shadow replied :
I am that dependence
Who carried you on my back
On that day,
I am that compassion
 Who offered you a kingdom

At the archery test
In Varunabata
I am that determination
Who vested in your hands
The succession
Of Kuru-troops.
'Hastina, my mother!'
I was startled, groped in the dark
And caught hold of her lotus-feet...
'Leave me, leave me' :
I came into my sense
And saw she was Brushali, turned into a statue,
Holding my two hands.

## 43

*(The night before the war. The melody of Krishna's flute was heard from the other bank of the river, and on this side stood Karna...)*

At that other bank of *Hiranwati*
If this bamboo flute
Could play all through the night
And the trees far away
Would look more mysterious
In this misty darkness?
Would these floating clouds
Keep the messengers of Yama
Descending stealthily from the sky,
Hidden till break of dawn !

It's not that
I had not heard
Such a flute earlier!

Once, very early in the morning
Placing my hand on Brushali's shoulder
I had listened to this flute,
At Champa Nagari,
As I kissed her
She quickly turned aside
And said :
'Oh, it's not night any more,
See, it has lightened'.

Flute is flute
But the same flute gives varied expressions
Have I ever thought of it?
To an amorous lady
Sleeping in the laps
Of an impotent husband
And, to a father, who has lost his son
This flute speaks in different notes
Those, alive, are not seen
To a girl in love
The few dead, lying on the ground, are not seen
To the soldiers heading for war
When this flute plays.

## 44

How much the people there
Care about the people living here.
That I do realise now, alone
On the bank of this river…
Only they descend
From the notes of the flute
When we get drowned

In the ocean of life's illusion
Their eyes look tearful
For scolding us sometime in the past
For unsettled obstinacy,
The dead children urge again,
Under this shady moonlight.

Ah! If they could speak
As they did on that day
They would insist
On not fighting this war
They would offer oblations to the gods
For my immortality.
If they knew
That this war is preordained
They would pat on the back
To buck up for the ordeal
Ah! If only they could speak.

Do the beloveds also come in veils
On the night before the war
After the family members are asleep?
Does the flute share
The sound of their disturbed foot-steps
At the distant *bastis*
In the midnight before each war?
The war is yet to start,
Why does it chill my body and mind
Someone's touch
( Is she my wife?)
In this quiet light of stars,
Do you know
Oh, flute !!

## 45

I shall have to fight tomorrow
To straighten the heads
Of all men
Who walk with down-cast faces
Under the sky…
I shall have to be
A bit of unmindful smile
On the lonely lips of the tender girl
Returning home at the day-end
With a fish-basket on her head.
Being wicks
In all the abandoned earthen-lamps
I shall fight against the forty-nine winds[1] tomorrow
At the village-border.

I shall pick up my weapons
At the right time
From whoever I like
In that battle-field…
With purpose I will prepare
The black bamboo sticks
Kept on the old-upper shelves
I will make *Brahmastra*
Out of the rusted *Dashara-sword*
In the hands of Devi…
Remember
Where my tear and my distress meet
There and there only
Exists my *Kurukshetra*
Forever…!

---
1 *(49 winds- violent breathing before death)*

Tomorrow...
And tomorrow for sure
For little Hastinas
Of little common men
I will offer my blood, my breath..

Tomorrow...
Then, why should I fight??
It's for this only :
That the tree has given me *Dabala Kathi*[2]
To my innocence
To my thirst
River has given water,
And birds have given consolations
To my defeats...!

And if I don't fight
Tell me, how do I answer
The queries of the trees and rivers and the birds!

## 46

I will fight for that land
That gave me the first dust
For my playhouse...
I will fight for that star
That gave me my first dream
In my boyhood days...
For that star I must fight...
For me,
Yes, for me
I will fight of course
The battle of tomorrow.

---

2 *The play material like cricket-bat*

Whether there is a crown
To adorn my head or not,
Whether it is at Kurukshetra
Or on the bank of the Ganga.
Whether there is someone behind me
For support
Or there is loneliness all around me
I must fight my battle tomorrow.

In the memory of my son
Who left me alone
I shall build my power and valour
With two drops of tear
Taken from my mother's eyes
I shall make my ear-rings, robbed from me.
Is there any other need of a defensive armour?
For my chest protected
By the embrace of my wife !!

Tell me
Were not many a Duryodhan
Born somewhere
Many a Arjun since time immemorial,
Kunti and Krishna likewise
Have I ever fought on behalf of any of them ?

But this time
I must fight the battle tomorrow
Not for any others
But for myself, for myself alone.
Arjun is just a pretext
And so are
Krishna
Hastina
And the Kurukshetra.

## 47

*(The afternoon before war, anxieties of Karna)*

The direction in which
 Those two lone cranes flew away once
Touching the dark clouds
Will be vibrating tomorrow
With the jingling of weapons
The gentle birds will fly away
In fear
Leaving behind their accustomed nests
At bathing *ghat*
Will be heard the sound of breaking bangles
(Not of earthen pitchers gurgling in water)
At the land
Where *Pururaba* and *Urvashi* met,
Will dance the headless trunks of innocent warriors.

Brusha ! Just see
How this Sebati plant bears
Countless little buds
That shall bloom tomorrow...
May be the branches of these trees
Will be crowded tomorrow
With the chirping of too many birds
The conch at the ceremony of a new Almanack
Will be heard in the evening
From distant villages
Brighter moon-light shall flood
Every nook and corner
Of the mysterious forest
Like unending dreams,
But a lot many people,

Known to us,
Either in Hastina
Or in Indraprastha
Will not be there anymore tomorrow.

The war only takes away.
Even the visitors come back home
With empty hands
To live the rest of their meaningless lives,
That are like the residues of food
Left on the leaf-plate
Just after the eater gets up.
All that the war leaves behind
Is some vacant spaces
Some empty rivers,
Some dead-eyes, some deserted land.

The war comes nevertheless
Without paying heed to the dragon-flies, the butterflies
And the melancholic sunsets,
Ignoring
The whisperings of God
War comes
As a coma in the middle of a sentence.

War comes and goes…
Just when one remembers the most precious
Events of life
The National Flag shrouds the face.

## 48

After bidding farewell, waving my hands
To every sunset of my life,
That is drawing to a close
In lovelessness and jealousy
After every footstep of mine
That has been cursed
I never knew
So much of pleasure
Was there for me in store.

While coming back home
In the late afternoon
Wife Brushali stood holding the roof
With a sulking face
Like rest of the darkness of night
About to end,
The vermilion
In the parting of her hair
Looked like the rising-sun…

The temptation of looking back at life
Again and again
Dazzled on her marble-white wrist
Like red bangles…
Who knows who had gathered and why
The white oysters of her unforgettable love
At the lonely shore
Of her lonesome smile…!!

On the other side,
The activities

Of sons, expert in archery and horse-riding,
Is seen
The funeral-pyre
That burnt long ago
Is indistinctly visible
Without any pain in it
The old wound feels painful
When touched
Oh, dear friend !!

## 49
*(Memories of wife Brusha and Krishnaa in the battle field)*

You are outside of your world
And
Me mine, all through the ages…
Like one feels
When I am neither in sleep nor awake,
As if you are a dawn
Of a hermitage nearby
And I am
An evening of a distant hill…
Just tell me, how difficult it is really
To separate the night from a day?

In which way
This cruel battle field,
Soaked by the blood and flesh of near and dear ones
Is better than the fortune of
Sitting by your thin round lac-dye on your feet,
And flying away and coming back to you again?
Holding weapons in hesitant hands
Killing others first

And then the fellow men
And to earn thereby the futile glory –
Which fighter would crave for this ?

Tell me
If all the alternatives
Of this meaningless blood-shed
Have been exhausted in the course of time ?
If wounded by your warm fragrant breath
I fly away and relentlessly return to you
Like the ever-fascinated bee
Why won't history
Deem it virility on my part ?

Ridden with many a doubt
This poor destitute
For him you and Brusha are not different
With saris and ear-ring
Of the same colour
You both are illusions alike !
Are you
My unsuccessful love
Being Krishnaa in place of Brusha
Uttered again and again
On my tongue ?

As you go rumbling
In grey-dark distant cloud
The thunder of early *Ashadha*
In my blood…
And I am like the excited plumage of a peacock
On some hilltop amidst dense-trees
Leaning towards you
Life after life…

Tell me still then
Why does a void thin like a sesame-seed
Separate those moments of ours
On the point of being absorbed into each other.
Tell me
Why am I at the same time
Someone who is crazy for war
And also one who runs away from war.

## 50
*(Discussion on war in countryside)*

None for the sake of Hastina
Each one fights his own battle
A word has gone around since yesterday…
'What does a state mean?'
Neither Bhisma understood
Nor Drona woke up
Poor Karna
What war he would fight
In a state of being and non-being !

Just listen! When in the hands of enemy
What's the point in setting a condition?
When you've taken salt at his place
You've to sing his praises
You can't eat your cake
And have it too
What kind of war is it ?
If you must fight, fight without fear and favour.

Someone said : Brothers !
Bhishma is alright in a way
Look at Drona

What did he do for the state
Except killing his own enemy
Drupada ?
Another commented...
Be he Drona
He is a man after all
Hearing the shocking news
Of his young son's death
Which father would engage himself in a fight ?

Someone else said :
Where is remedy for that
When one is aware of the fact
Aswatthama is immortal
And ask
'Oh, Krishna !
Oh, Jujhesthi !
Is Aswatthama dead or alive?'

Spectators are spectators
Down the ages.
They always whispher after a thing has happened
But my father says :
These spectators
Are the friends of the state
In times of need,
Not the soldiers
Nor the generals.

Returning to the camp
After sun-down
I think in solitude :
What does a state truly mean?
Does it mean some Blocks, Tehsils

Some *Mandals*, some *Janapadas*
Some cities, rivers
Some churches, some temples ?
For which
There is a mace at one side
And a *Gandiva* at the other?
For which
Kurus at one side
And Pandavas at the other?

## 51

*(Kurukshetra : To overcome his sense of inferiority caused by the eulogy for Partha by Salya, Karna's eagerness to listen to the slander of Partha)*

Owls hoot, dogs bark.
Drums sound and banners murmur
One can also hear the faint subdued cries
And war-cry for fight...
But how I wish
I could hear someone slander against Partha
And Partha only...

Let Partha's slander
Come from all directions
From the premises of court
From the lips of children going to school
From the chirping of birds
And from the terrible rattling sound
Of the chariot driven by Salya !!

If I could hear the slanderous words
In the stealthy darkness

Coming from the neighbourhood of brothers
Would I be hearing Partha's slander
From the never-ending talk
Of the couple meeting after many days
From the faraway flute
Playing at intervals
From the songs of Yogis wandering
With begging-bowls
From the half-asleep, half-awake
Army-camp !
I shall offer *Kamadhenu* cow
To the persons who slander Partha
I shall offer all the water-lilies
Plucked from my uncle's pond
Shall offer my pearl necklace
To Partha's slanderer
And a palace, bright as moonlight
To live in.
If the slanderer is a male
I shall offer him a million women of divine beauty
And if a female
For her, I shall trace out a divine male.
To one who would scandal Partha
I shall offer a million elephants and horses,
The whole of the earth
Except Hastina.

To Partha's slanderer
I shall offer all my skills of archery
All my virtues of this life
And of previous lives, if needed
Rest of the kisses of my wife meant for me.
Shall offer the span of my life

Balance in hand till death
I must give in time
My unmaterialised love,
To those who slander Partha.
I promise !!

## 52

*(The battle-field : Salya shows Karna the chariot of Arjun)*

Said Salya : Oh! King of Anga
See, there is the *Devadalan*, the chariot of Arjuna
A fitting reply to the challenge you threw once to him
For the Charioteer's fight one to one
Your vanished fear
That floated and settled once
In the winds of Dwaitavana,
Those restless hateful words
That one day mocked at you
And returned half-way
At the border of *Virat Nagar*,

An upright occasion
To repay all the debts of Hastina
That awaits you…

Before I had a clear view of Arjuna
What act of revenge occurs before me
Whose severed head is this
Crying out 'father', Oh father,
Dazzling the earth and the heaven
Dropped from among the clouds
Like a meteor ?
Whose slain head is this ?

That sticks to the arrow-point
Like a soft *shirish* flower
Struck down by the wind ?

No, why should he be Brusasena !
My dear son *Bishikeshan* ?
He has promised to his mother
To return in the evening
With the necklace and the ear-rings
Of the dead soldiers...
He has promised to his grand-mother
He would tell her in the dark moonless night
About the incomparable happenings
Of this fierce fight,
My child is not so
That he would deny his mother's words.

Salya ! my able charioteer
My friend, my brother
Why are you so quiet ?
Tell me,
This lotus-head is not of my Brusa...
Tell my brother, why are you so silent?
To a father that has lost his way
The happy tidings about his young son.

Oh! King of Madra
Are you angry with me?
Virtuous(?) in this battlefield of Kurukshetra
Touching this bow I swear
I shall never tell a word
That might hurt you
Till I am alive.

In this tearful battle field
Is there any other except you
Whom I shall call my own ?
Before whom shall I confide
My earnest suppressed longings ?
The branch on which I sat
After flying and flying
Broke
Is there anyone who knows it
More than you,
The last resources
Of my life about to set !!

## 53
*(Laments of maddened Karna after the death of Brushasena)*

You don't say anything, Salya,
Then, this is Brushasena !
A relieved Arjuna : Then, this is Brushasena.
My left eye blinks : of course this is
Brushasena.

But why ?
On what compulsion
What obligation
He left me alone
At this stage
Full of distress !
Where is the answer to that ?
Oh, my grief-stricken soldiers!
Go, bring back my Brushasena
From the uncertain outcome
Of the battle.

Tell him! All his play-mates
Killed in this battle
I will bring them back to life.
Tell him ! I'll seek those back
All the oyster-shells
And coconut-shells
Lost from his infancy.

Tell him
I shall bring back
All the humming of bees
All the colours of the butter-flies
All the first flights of birds
All the evenings of ribbed-gourd flowers
Disappeared from his faded memory.

Oh, King of Madra !
Return now the chariot
From the cremation-ground of sons
Now turn the chariot round and go
To the impatient void
Waiting as an image at the door-sill
Announce in country to country
*Trilokas* and *Trikalas*
Basu is a war-deserter
Basu is a half-charioteer .

No, no… King of Madra
Let's not go back
Now run the chariot to the front…
Now let the chariot swallow up
Partha, the son of Pandu
Krishna, the son of Brushni

And whole of the battle field
Not only the battlefield
The whole of Indraprastha.
Not only whole of Indraprastha
But the sky above, the underground
And the ten directions
The whole of the world.
As the banyan leaf reaches beyond
The dissolution
And the life goes beyond the domain of death
As the sand-storm spreads over the sea-shore
And the consequence of actions done in past life
Extends to the present !

Who is there to succeed Karna?
Karna has no past nor future
Karna means Karna is here
And that is that !

## 54
*(Overwhelmed with grief at the death of his son, Karna uses the Naga-weapon Aimed at Arjuna but misses the target.)*

It seemed as if
A blood-splashed hand of a boy
Pushed the arrow to a slightly higher level,
The hand familiar for years.

The hand that has touched
In many an indifferent afternoon
My beard grown over time without care,
Like a jasmine-creeper
This hand has entwined

The sal-neck of Brushali,
Warm as a bird's belly
After worship in the early morning
My Radhi Bou
Had tied the *Surya-Kabacha*
On this hand,
By this hand
The plucked feather
Of an innocent dragon-fly that escaped
Just while it was being caught,
The last dust
Of the play-house
That was made and broken
By this hand…

The Naga-weapon, freed from my quiver
After tearing through *Kapi Ketana*
Disappeared
Into my barren future
As the gusty tree
Swept by the fury of the storm
Settles still and quiet
Govinda as well as *Govinda, the second*[3]
Leaning down a little
Remained sedate
Like a frill of casuarina.
By the sea-shore
Under an unending sky,
Was separated like
A tuft of flower of the crown
Shook a little
As the branch is shaken

---

3  Duryodhan is also addressed as Mana-Govinda

While the bird starts to fly,
A strand of unrest
Startled at the string of my bow…

Whose call is it
Heard from across a distance
Father, come…come!
Standing there
Beyond the reach of the eyes
Wet with tears
Who are these two children
Abhimanyu ?
Ghatotkacha ?
Salya,
Now, take back the chariot
I am coming
Tell Managovinda
If it was not at that time…
Even now, at this time
Not keeping his words.
A clueless general is going back
To that place,
From where one never returns.

Go on my Brusha, my son
 Walk on…
How far they have gone
Those two playful brothers…
The seven horses
Are getting restive
At the sun-down behind the hill
The day is drawing to a close
Oh, my child… walk on …!

## 55

*[From the border of the city is heard a great deal of noise.
Brushali is asking a house maid]*

Maid !
What is that noise we hear from afar?
Go and see…
If prince Brushasena is
Returning victorious from the battle field
If so, why the victory-conch of
Hastina is not heard ?
Why doesn't flutter the flag in the wind?

Maid! Just drive away this crow
From the wall-stand of the palace
Oh, my dear crow
Fly away
My son has gone to the battle-field
When he returns, I promise,
There shall be sweets for you.

He is shy by nature, you know
Why do you crowd around
Get off his way
My dear one may jump out of the gathering
And hang about my neck in fondness
He might have gone without food the whole day
Leave him
Let him rush into the kitchen,
And look at the containers
Hanging from the roof.

Move aside
Let me ask him
My dear, did you return alone,
Where is your father?
Is it right to go to the mass
Without getting inside the house
And without a word with me...
Tell me, my son
Who were delivered to the heaven
By your arrows!
Say, what honours were conferred on you
By the King of Hastina?

Move aside a little
Heat of the sun
And heat of the battle
He is tired...
Let him get a little air
No, don't wake him up
After a sound sleep
He would get up by himself
It may be after a short while
Or after an age...!!

## 56
*(The dead body of Brusasena is brought in a coffin.*
*A stunned Brushali at the door-step)*

Mother!
Have you not heard
From father,
Sometimes chariots break down
In the battle-field!
Some return on foot

Some in coffins!
Have you gone mad, Mother!
Why do you stand at the door-step
Like a log of wood!

Look…look, Mother!
How has your son returned today
From Kurukshetra, after the war!


When I went to fight
You had told me
To come, wearing the scarfs of dead heroes
On my shoulder
A scarf is a small thing, Mother!
Look,
How your son has come back
Wearing the flag of his nation…

He has left behind him
At the battle-field
His quiver full of arrows
The bow that shakes the earth
Hasn't he done the right thing?
Those are not mere arrows, mother!
Those are the sorrowful-cries
 Lifeless things
How could they have wiped out
The tears rolling down other's eyes!

Mother!
Would you be angry with me?
I have forgotten

To bring the ear-rings
And the waist-scarfs
Of the soldiers killed in the battle…
Mother!
Do you think those are so valuable?
Open my fist and see
What I have brought for you
Have brought…
A handful of blood-soaked dust
Of my country
In which
All my evenings
All my mornings
The whole of my infancy and boyhood
Have turned grey.

Mother! Don't bother
No more shall I tell you,
The stories of the battle
Leaning on your ears,
How the heroes from the enemy camp
Desperately cry just before death,
How a robust crow snatches
The eyes of a young soldier, fresh as a lotus
And flies to the branch of a tree.
How the frightful maddened horse
Crushes under its hooves
The charioteer whom it had carried so far
How the cries and calls
Merge together in the air
How the bragging of the morning
Flies away in the evening
Riding on the vulture's wings.

Mother! Henceforth
You will sleep all by yourself
Undisturbed.
The bare-moon
Like the hands of a newly-widowed woman
Will set as soon as it touches you.

Mother!
So many have gathered round me
My body, smeared with turmeric by you,
Now lies hidden under heaps of flowers
On my body.
Before the *Diya* that you had lighted
In the *Puja room* dims and goes out
Come and welcome me
With hymns and calls of bigul
And cries of *Hulahuli*
Before I get buried under mourning
Do offer *Akshata Duba*
On the route along which
My body would be carried
Mother!
Adorn me with the sandal-paste that you have kept
On the golden plate…
And say in my ears, with all your heart
For the last time :
Glory to Hastinapur
Glory to Basushena !!

## 57

The wheel of my chariot
Got stuck into the ground
Of tear, decayed water and rotten flesh
And was lost
An undesignated name
In the open mouth of eternity…

Millions of golden *champak*
In her worship-basket,
One who doesn't have so rare a mother,
Can one say he really has
A path decked with flowers?
In the mud of my orphan birth
My reckless living
And disgraceful identity
The wheel of my chariot
Got buried…
Where is that aristocratic set-up
Of noble family history
To hold high the dusty loft of my fate
The damaged axis of my chariot?

Eyeing with greed the torn intestine
And the entrails of the carcass
The watchful crow and the vulture
Beat their wings
At this unusual happening…
The plain and open clouds
That have played with dust together
Since childhood
Designed an illusion of evening

In the west
Blocking the way of the sun!

Walking barefoot
I looked at the wheel
That lay buried in earth
With one eye
And the opponent by the other
Ah! The jewelled ear-rings
Of Basudev,
Looked like an impotent anger of a landlord
Terrified by the tenant's agitation,
And I saw
A big non-poisonous snake
With an unfrightful hiss
Rushing towards the harmless screaming
Of innocent birds
And I saw too
The unvanquished(?) Drona's disciple
The Great Archer, a poor imitation of Partha(!)
Slowly fading away.

While placing my palm
On the wheel of my chariot
Stuck in the earth
I realised today
In some Kurukshetra or other
How much unethical conduct
Is scared of propriety?
How much the crown
Is afraid of a vow made?
How much the *Ishwara* with a thousand name
Is afraid of the nameless
Who never wants to live with another's identity?

## 58

Goodbye my dear battle-field
Now lying rotten with the blood
Of millions of innocent soldiers
Goodbye
All the rivers and mountains and forests
All the darkness and lights of this universe!

All my enemies and all my opponents
Have taken their birth
Before I was born, I know…
My poor fate
Had already been covered by rocks
From my mother's womb:
I know of course.

My first enemy:
My mother
Ah! The poor and miserable
Because of her foolishness
Second :
My teacher who taught me war-crafts
Alas! Because of his ego of casteism.
Third:
Bhisma, Vidur, Drona, Krupa…shame!
For their helplessness.
Sakuni, the other evil-doer
Born out of treachery…
Arjun, Bhima are my enemies;
Unfortunates! For their ignorance…
And my enemy Draupadi
Since I was the cause of her ruin…

From among my handful of friends
You are one – oh, you earth
But at this crucial hour
Of this unappeasing war
Why did you take away
Your reliable crust?

I don't bother
Who forgot me no matter where
My only regret
Is that you too left Radheya
At the last moment
Oh! you earth!

Oh! my hand of noble descent
Offering oblations
To the infinite.
Oh! my hideous hand
That instigated the assault of Panchali
Patting on my thigh
Oh! my brutal hand that took part
In the death
Of innocent Abhimanyu.
Now ah! How ordinary
Are you of Karna, now?

## 59

Dazed at this destined fall of mine
Ah! my deprived lot
In all the times – present, past and future
Never retreat even a bit
Keep on fighting...
I will return to that side
That stands defeated
A million times.
Basusena stands committed
To you, to you only.

Oh! my contempt and love
Farewell to you
Oh! the rest of my dreams
And, rest of my war
I bid you farewell today
Oh, my orphan sighs
And, my poor drops of tear
I take leave of you
Oh, the weeping lilly and the setting moon
Farewell to you
I seek forgiveness
If I have hurt anyone's feelings...

Oh, friend of Arjun
In the heart of the solar-disc
Accept my last salute
That I offer
"To meditate ever-Narayan
Who sits at the core of the solar disc
On the lotus seat

Golden embodiment, adorned with
Conch and wheel
Ornamented with armlets, shark-shaped
Ear-ring, crown and necklace...!!"

## 60
*(Laments of Draupadi at the funeral fire of Karna)*

Oh! the eldest Kaunteya
My first husband
How much do you sleep
Wake up... rise.
All are asleep
Trees, rivers, planets and the space
This night is meant for us
Only for us...

After a number of birth and a number of death
This lonely night is granted to us.
Will this night,
Very personal and private,
Get spent in mere sleep of yours?

Wake up... wake up.
Oh! the first dream of my youth
My silent widowhood
Rise up
From death
From mortality
And from the funeral pyre
Oh! The first Pandava
Oh! my mother Yajna
Would you be quiet
The first bangle and the first vermilion
Of your daughter is burnt!

Oh, my love
This night is not like the other one
That evading my glance
You would go away playfully
Towards the river bank
And would avenge the whole of your virility
Because of my chiding
That was beyond my control!!

## 61

Oh! are you getting up…
I have made this bridal night
With all my love
Have made the bed of bright moon-light
Have hung the frills of twinkling stars
And other crafts that match the occasion.

Since our very birth
We are like two drops of tears
Rolling down in opposite directions
Under the hazy thin mist of net
Neither I to you
Nor you to me
Say 'wait'!

Say by all means if you want to,
Let me speak of mine
The sorrows that I could not share with others
Let the night deepen
Amidst our incompatible loneliness.

What shall I do
When night gets deeper
Why are you silent?
Why don't you ask me in a whisper – 'what'?
I'd implore your embrace
Return me my son who is dead
And you
My naughty butterfly
You will flit about
From place to place,
Flying and sitting here and there,
And will make me just restless.

Why don't you listen to me
Are you really cross with me?
Aim-test was forbidden for you
On principle
Since it was known to the people
That you were a son of a charioteer then...
To wake you up
What other way was left for me
Except making you angry?

A woman by birth and fate
Fickle in intelligence
"I am a swan
And you are a mere crow"
For that only I said.
While serving meal
At the Maya palace
Sari dropped from my chest
Ah! what coolness in your eyes
So did I utter...

"I am the offerer
And you the beggar"

Do you mind my saying so
 Since that day?

In the dawning night
Of my dishevelled hair
Oh! my distant morning star
 You rise now!
I might be your last wife
But, you're for sure my first paramour!!

### Black Eagle Books

www.blackeaglebooks.org
info@blackeaglebooks.org

Black Eagle Books, an independent publisher, was founded as a nonprofit organization in April, 2019. It is our mission to connect and engage the Indian diaspora and the world at large with the best of works of world literature published on a collaborative platform, with special emphasis on foregrounding Contemporary Classics and New Writing.

www.ingramcontent.com/pod-product-compliance
Lightning Source LLC
Chambersburg PA
CBHW060616080526
44585CB00013B/859